OUR FAMILY BOOK of LIFE

REV. HUGH TASCH, O.S.B. AND
REV. NORBERT SCHAPPLER, O.S.B.
MONKS OF CONCEPTION ABBEY

CALLIGRAPHY BY
DAVID MEKELBURG

THE PRINTERY HOUSE
OF CONCEPTION ABBEY   CONCEPTION, MISSOURI 64433

Imprimatur
  † John J. Sullivan, D.D.
     Bishop of Kansas City-St. Joseph

Imprimi potest
  † Jerome Hanus, O.S.B.
     Abbot of Conception Abbey

TABLE OF CONTENTS

FOREWORD

From the earliest days of Christianity, the family has played a special role in handing on the faith to each succeeding generation. Jesus himself was subject to Mary and Joseph: in the midst of his family he grew in wisdom, in stature, and in favor with God and men (Luke 2:52).

The great saints of Christian history understood that the family could be the place where the Christian faith was concretely experienced. There parents could proclaim the word of God. The family could pray and sing together. Hospitality to strangers and care for the needy could be exercised. By its example and its concern, the family could become an agent of evangelization and reconciliation. For these and other reasons, St. John Chrysostom and St. Augustine repeatedly exhorted the Christian people to "make their houses into churches of God."

The Fathers of the Second Vatican Council continued this tradition. "Parents by word and example are the first heralds of the faith to their children. The family should be thought of as a *domestic church*" (Constitution on the Church, 11).

If families in our day are to be conscious of their potential as Christian churches in miniature, a greater understanding of the riches of Christian faith must be fostered. This *Book of Life* is an attempt to encourage such growth in faith. The family that uses it will appreciate the importance of the sacraments as moments in the life of grace. In keeping a record of these important acts of Christian faith, the members of this family will be writing its own history. By God's grace and power, may the history of each Christian family, of each church in miniature, be one where human love and concern reflect the Good News of God's love for all people.

Abbot Jerome Hanus, O.S.B.
Conception Abbey
June 7, 1983

FAMILY USE OF THE BOOK OF LIFE

The victors shall go clothed in white. I will never erase their names from the book of the living, but will acknowledge them in the presence of my Father and his angels. . . Only those shall enter heaven whose names are inscribed in the book of the living by the Lamb.

Revelation 3:5; 21-27

According to this text of St. John, the Book of Life is a sacred sign of God's love and fidelity. Those whose names are written in this Book have entered the kingdom of his Son, the Lamb of God. These shall inherit eternal life.

Our Family Book of Life is a small symbol of that heavenly scroll of which St. John speaks. Its pages offer Christian families an occasion for building their spirituality upon Christ and his Church. The sacraments and other liturgical events are at the center of our religious encounters with the Lord. This *Family Book of Life* is a sacred reminder of that center.

In *Our Family Book of Life* all of the great sacramental celebrations of the family are to be recorded. This book is meant to be a constant companion for life's pilgrimage, a pilgrimage on the way to the wedding feast of the Lamb.

The plan for each section of *Our Family Book of Life*:
1. An appropriate text from the Bible, accompanied by an artistic symbol.
2. Two pages of commentary relating the liturgical event to Christian family life.
3. Record blanks, six in number, each providing for the desired information.
4. Pages for select photographs. Only photographs of a religious nature are to be entered, those taken on the occasion itself. *Our Family Book of Life* is not merely a photo album. It is a memorial of our spiritual journey to the fullness of Jesus' kingdom. And that journey is our life in the Church and its liturgy.

We suggest that the entries be made with due religious spirit. If they are made carelessly or at inopportune times, when few members of the family are present, the book will fail to teach and inspire. Such a matter should be a memorable event in the life of the family. Invite everyone, parents and children, to be present, for the joy is a family joy.

We hope *Our Family Book of Life* becomes a sacred object in your home. This suggests a number of practices during the course of the year. On the greater feasts, for instance, the book could be given a more prominent place in the living room. Easter is, of course, the traditional feast of Baptism and its renewal within the total parish community. On this day, then, the book might be opened upon a table, displaying the baptismal section. During Lent, perhaps, the sacraments of Reconciliation could be viewed; and pages for the Eucharist on the feast of the Body and Blood of Christ, or on Holy Thursday.

But perhaps more importantly, *Our Family Book of Life* can be made the focal point of family celebrations. The anniversaries of our own baptisms, confirmations, marriages, etc., are sacred days for each of us. It would be well for each family to embellish such days with its own inventive celebrations, gathered in prayer and simple fellowship around these commemorative pages.

In the back of this book is a section for genealogical records. It is provided as an additional help to relate your human family and human roots to your sublime dignity as a family of God.

Parents eager to help their children in understanding the religious meaning of this *Family Book of Life* will frequently explain the two texts from the *Book of Revelation* found at the beginning and end of this book. They will explain that this book is not only a register of our holy membership in the life-activities of the Church on earth but it is as well a profound image of the heavenly citizenship that is opened up to us. Our life in Christ is a foretaste of that eternal life which awaits us; and we shall enter heaven one day because we have been faithful to the Lamb's *Book of Life* during our years of Christian pilgrimage and service upon earth.

THE VICTORS SHALL GO
clothed in white. I will
never erase their names +
from THE BOOK OF LIFE,
but will acknowledge them
in the presence of my Father
and his angels. + REVELATION 3:5

THIS IS A GREAT SACRAMENT;

I mean that it refers to Christ and the Church.

EPHESIANS 5:32

3

ON the____day of_____, ____,

_____and_____,

wedded each other in Christ.

_____was the Church's

witness as we conferred this sacrament upon

each other.

WE offered the body and blood of Christ

to the Father, and with that sacred victim

we offered to God our entire married life.

We shared together in the eucharistic

communion in order that our human love

might be sanctified by the Spirit.

Ministering as best man and bridesmaid

were_____and_____.

Thus they too witnessed to the holy union

into which we have entered.

A HOLY covenant has been celebrated, an

irrevocable and mutual consent. This we

have freely and joyfully bestowed upon each other. We resolve to build our family life upon the sublime dignity we have received through the sacrament of marriage.

OUR union as husband and wife is a sacred image of the intimate union between Christ and his Church. Through the grace of this liturgy, the husband is for his wife an image of Christ, and the wife is for her husband an image of the Church. In our mutual love we realize that in truth we love Christ in each other. For we are a miniature of that great mystery which is Christ dwelling among his people.

OURS shall be a life-long pursuit of holiness through a faithful and fruitful love promoting the kingdom of God upon earth. May our fidelity never waver, but rather deepen with the years by the blessings of this holy day.

Wedding Photographs

Wedding Photographs

7

THROUGH BAPTISM
into Christ's death+
we were buried with
Him so that we too
might live a new life.

ROMANS 6:4

BAPTISM IS THE FIRST SACRAMENT of Christian initiation. Through water and the Holy Spirit all of Adam's children are freed from Satan's power and possession. ❖ They are born a second time, created anew into a life truly divine. ❖❖❖❖❖❖❖❖❖❖❖❖ A MOTHER brings forth her child to natural life. Mother Church brings forth children ❖ to a life in Christ Jesus. Thus formed into ❖❖ God's people they obtain forgiveness of sin ❖ and the dignity of children divinely adopted. LED through the doors of baptism, all the members of our human family enter the ❖❖ kingdom of God, the Church. They are built into a house where God dwells, consecrated into a holy people and a royal priesthood. ❖

THIS rebirth in the Spirit is an entrance into the Paschal Mystery of Jesus. With him we are buried, with him we rise to a new life. The joy of resurrection is ours, a sharing in eternal life while yet in this mortal flesh. As Moses led the people through the Red Sea, so does Christ lead his newly formed disciples into the Land of Promise, both now and in the Age to come.

FOR THE Christian mother and father, baptism is a source of great joy. Their children are now drawn into the family of God. Thus is Christian rebirth a family sacrament on three levels: it sanctifies the home, it enlarges the family of parish and diocese, and it unites the newly baptized with the worldwide Body of Christ. Most grandly of all, it calls the human family to the ultimate resurrection: life in heaven.

The New Life of BAPTISM received in our Family

Name _____

Birth _____ Rebirth _____

Minister _____

Godfather _____

Godmother _____

Church _____

City _____ State _____

Name _____

Birth _____ Rebirth _____

Minister _____

Godfather _____

Godmother _____

Church _____

City _____ State _____

Name _____

Birth _____ Rebirth _____

Minister _____

Godfather _____

Godmother _____

Church _____

City _____ State _____

Name _____

Birth _____ Rebirth _____

Minister _____

Godfather _____

Godmother _____

Church _____

City _____ State _____

Name _____

Birth _____ Rebirth _____

Minister _____

Godfather _____

Godmother _____

Church _____

City _____ State _____

Name _____

Birth _____ Rebirth _____

Minister _____

Godfather _____

Godmother _____

Church _____

City _____ State _____

Baptismal Photographs

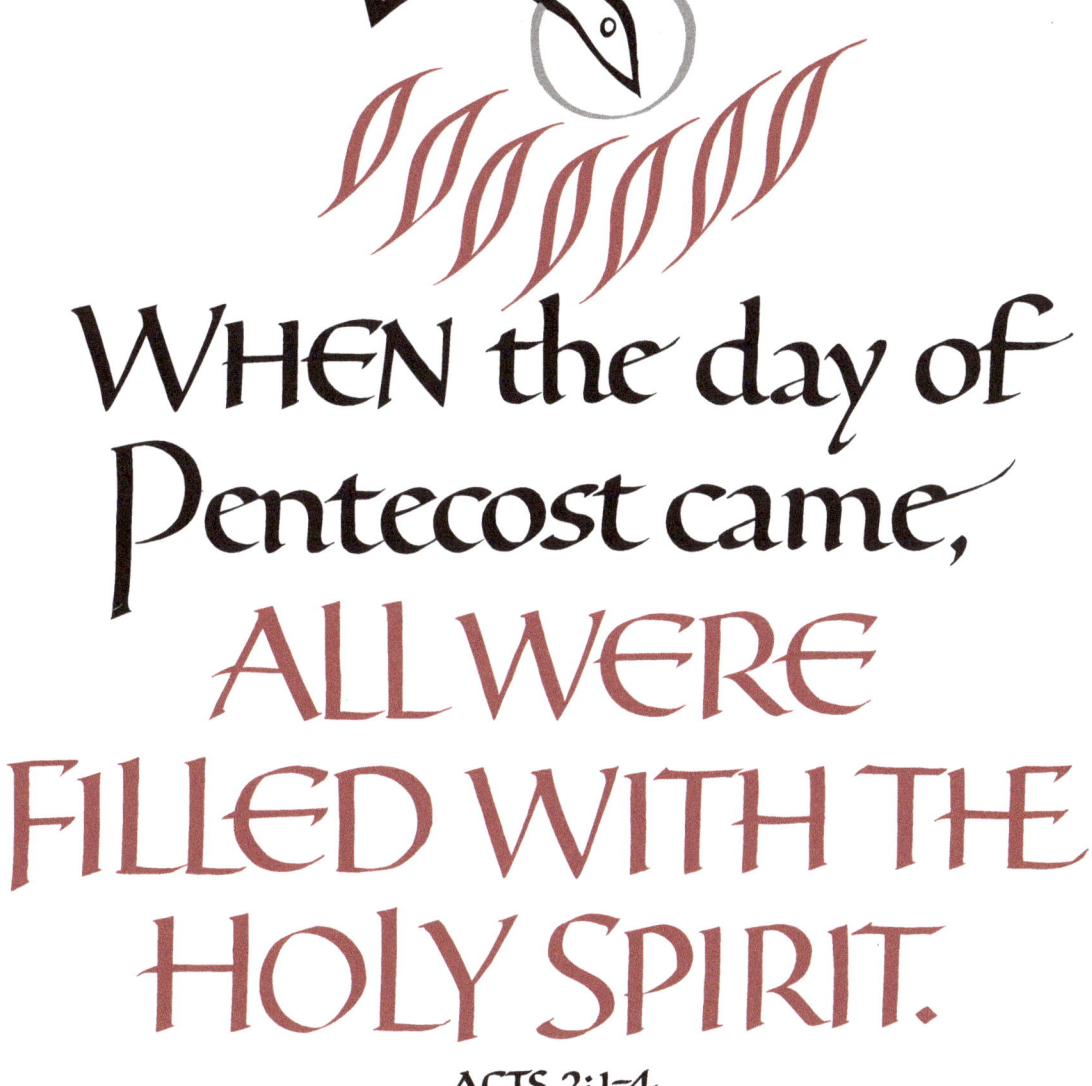

WHEN the day of
Pentecost came,
ALL WERE
FILLED WITH THE
HOLY SPIRIT.

ACTS 2:1–4

IN THE RITE OF CONFIRMATION ✝ we celebrate the second phase of Christian initiation, intimately connected with baptism. Just as Jesus was anointed and consecrated by the descent of the Spirit after his baptism in the Jordan, so the pentecostal Spirit is bestowed more fully upon those who have already been raised to new life at the baptismal font. IN baptism we receive the forgiveness of sin ❖ and the adoption as children of God. Through the sacrament of confirmation we receive the inexpressible gift which is the Holy Spirit. ❖ Henceforward, we are bound more closely and more completely to the Church. We are likewise more firmly obliged to witness to our faith ❖ before others both by word and by worthiness of life. More deeply, confirmation hallows the Christian believer more fully as a member of the priestly people. It consecrates the ❖ ❖ ❖

baptized for the noble liturgy of offering the eucharistic sacrifice in union with Christ. ❖ THE sacred minister of confirmation extends his hand over the initiate. He anoints the ❖ head with chrism, the holiest of oils. Thus is enacted a solemn bestowal of the Gift of the Spirit. On the night before Jesus underwent his passion, he promised to send the Paraclete who would abide with us forever. And after his resurrection he assured his disciples: "You will receive power when the Holy Spirit comes down upon you. Then you are to be my witnesses." ❖ BY the sacred oil we are therefore consecrated. In the power of that Spirit we are enabled to give fitting worship to God. We are likewise summoned to proclaim to the world the ❖ ❖ mighty works of God. Confirmation is our sanctification, our receiving of divine power, and our being sent forth upon a mission ❖ ❖ to all whom the Lord would have us serve.

The spiritual strength of CONFIRMATION received in our Family

Name _____

Confirmation Name _____

Date _____

Minister _____

Sponsor _____

Church _____

City _____ State _____

Name _____

Confirmation Name _____

Date _____

Minister _____

Sponsor _____

Church _____

City _____ State _____

Name_____

Confirmation Name_____

Date_____

Minister_____

Sponsor_____

Church_____

City_____ State_____

Name_____

Confirmation Name_____

Date_____

Minister_____

Sponsor_____

Church_____

City_____ State_____

Name _____

Confirmation Name _____

Date _____

Minister _____

Sponsor _____

Church _____

City _____ State _____

Name _____

Confirmation Name _____

Date _____

Minister _____

Sponsor _____

Church _____

City _____ State _____

ALL·THOSE·WHO· feed on my flesh and drink my blood remain in me and I in them. JOHN 6:56

PARENTS LONG FOR THE DAY WHEN, as father and mother, they can lead ❖ ❖ ❖ their children to the table of the Lord. ❖ The eucharist is the great and final step of the initiation process for all of his disciples. FROM the earth come bread and the ❖ ❖ fruit of the vine. It is the desire of the ❖ Risen Messiah that all Christians partake frequently in holy communion with him, with all his saints in heaven and in this ❖ world, and even with the whole of creation redeemed by his blood. Eating and drinking together at the sacramental meal he has ❖ left us transforms us fully into his Church. THE BREAD of life and the cup of eternal salvation unite God and his people in an ineffable bond. By the consecrating prayer of thanksgiving the Holy Spirit sanctifies not only bread and wine, but even more wonder-

fully hallows the family of Christ. In a ❖ ❖
most mysterious fashion, the Church is the
eucharist and the eucharist is the Church. ❖

IN such divine and human ways, the death ❖
and rising of Jesus is celebrated, the holiness
of his people is accomplished, and a foretaste
of heaven itself are proclaimed and bestowed.
Gathered before the altar of Christ the High
Priest, the assembly of believers everywhere is
empowered to offer with him a pure sacrifice
of praise. The temple of heaven and our poor
human lives are here in profound unity. In
the holy banquet the new and eternal ❖ ❖ ❖
covenant is sealed. ❖ ❖ ❖ ❖ ❖ ❖ ❖ ❖ ❖ ❖ ❖ ❖

THERE is no greater communion with God
than this, nor is our love and faith shared ❖
anywhere more deeply than here. The Lord's
Supper is the focal point of our faith and
holy fellowship. ❖ ❖ ❖ ❖ ❖ ❖ ❖ ❖ ❖ ❖ ❖

EUCHARISTIC COMMUNION

shared in for the first time in our Family

Name _____

Date _____

Celebrant of Mass _____

Church _____

City _____ State _____

Name _____

Date _____

Celebrant of Mass _____

Church _____

City _____ State _____

Name _____

Date _____

Celebrant of Mass _____

Church _____

City _____ State _____

Name _____

Date _____

Celebrant of Mass _____

Church _____

City _____ State _____

Name _____

Date _____

Celebrant of Mass _____

Church _____

City _____ State _____

Name _____

Date _____

Celebrant of Mass _____

Church _____

City _____ State _____

WHOSE·SINS
you·shall·forgive,
+ they·are +
forgiven·them. JOHN 20:23

CHRIST, THE DIVINE PHYSICIAN, HEALS US by the forgiveness of sins. He does this in countless ways. Baptism first cleanses the children of Adam, and eucharistic communion restores our reconciliation with God. Prayer, too, leads to divine forgiveness – for ourselves and for those for whom we pray. Assisting the poor, ministering to those less fortunate, approaching humbly those we have hurt in any way in order to ask for pardon – all these are channels of God's forgiveness for our sins. BUT THE Savior has given us a special ❖ ❖ ❖ sacrament of reconciliation. For, although we have been made holy by the indwelling of Christ, we are ever in need of purification, ❖ continually pursuing repentance and renewal. Our human weakness is always with us. Thus do we approach God's bountiful mercy with

ongoing sorrow and regret. ❖ ❖ ❖ ❖ ❖ ❖ ❖ ❖ ❖ ❖ ❖
AT once more solemnly and more spiritually than in other liturgies, the sacrament of ❖ ❖ penance reveals God's gracious love for ❖ ❖ ❖ sinners. God desires to reconcile the world ❖ to himself in Christ. Thus did the Lord, after his resurrection, send the Spirit upon the ❖ ❖ apostles, appointing them to extend to ❖ ❖ ❖ humankind the grace of forgiveness in his name. EVERY sin is an offense against God and ❖ against our sisters and brothers. The sin of each person harms all the others. Therefore in the celebration of penance we come ❖ ❖ ❖ confidently to God's throne of grace, and we likewise pray for one another and ask ❖ ❖ ❖ mutually for pardon. We also come with hearts filled with thanksgiving: the faithfulness of Christ's healing power can never fail. To ❖ those who are contrite of heart, God is love.

The Healing
Sacrament of
RECONCILIATION
received
for the first time
in our Family

Name _____

Date _____

Confessor _____

Church _____

City _____ State _____

Name _____

Date _____

Confessor _____

Church _____

City _____ State _____

Name _____

Date _____

Confessor _____

Church _____

City _____ State _____

Name _____

Date _____

Confessor _____

Church _____

City _____ State _____

Name _____

Date _____

Confessor _____

Church _____

City _____ State _____

Name _____

Date _____

Confessor _____

Church _____

City _____ State _____

ARE THERE ANY SICK
among you? Let them ask
for the priests of the church
who in turn are to pray over
them, anointing them with oil
IN THE NAME OF THE LORD.

JAMES 5:14

WHILE JESUS WALKED AMONG US in his earthly ministry, he healed the sick by his earnest prayer and the laying on of hands. And by the power of his heavenly Father he declared:"Go now, your sins are forgiven."

ANOINTING of the sick is a sacrament of healing. It brings us today to the Lord's loving care for the infirm of body and spirit. Through the human ministry of priests and the gathering of the faithful in prayer, the Savior extends his healing power. The Church commends those who are ill to the suffering and glorified Lord, that he might raise them up and save them.

THE priest anoints the sick with holy oil; he likewise prays for healing. The Holy Spirit is thus bestowed, sins are forgiven, and, if God's providence has so planned, bodily health is restored. ❖❖❖❖❖❖❖❖❖❖❖❖❖❖❖❖❖❖

ANOINTING of the sick is a family ❖❖❖❖ sacrament. Frequently it is administered in the home, with mother and father, brother and sister present. Together the family prays for the loved one. Through this prayer of ❖ faith God may restore physical wholeness ❖ to the infirm. Yet divine wisdom may ordain otherwise. The Lord may choose to welcome his follower into eternal life. The sacrament then prepares the dying Christian for ❖❖ immediate entrance into heaven. An inner strength is so given that death itself cannot shake the profound faith that dwells in the heart.

THE death and resurrection of Christ ❖❖❖ bestow power. By our faith we are healed— both in this mortal life and in the Age to come.

The
comfort of the
ANOINTING
OF THE SICK
received
in our Family

Name _____

MINISTER	DATE
_____	_____
_____	_____
_____	_____
_____	_____

Name _____

MINISTER	DATE
_____	_____
_____	_____
_____	_____
_____	_____

*Name*_____

MINISTER   DATE

_____   _____

_____   _____

_____   _____

_____   _____

*Name*_____

MINISTER   DATE

_____   _____

_____   _____

_____   _____

_____   _____

Name_____

MINISTER	DATE
_____	_____
_____	_____
_____	_____
_____	_____

Name_____

MINISTER	DATE
_____	_____
_____	_____
_____	_____
_____	_____

THEY PRESENTED
these men to the
✝ apostles who first ✝
prayed over them
AND THEN IMPOSED
HANDS ON THEM.
ACTS 6:6

FROM APOSTOLIC TIMES WE HAVE traditionally been served by three orders of special ministry in the Church: the order of bishops, the order of priests, and the order of deacons. In our own day we have seen a renewed attention given to the office of deacon, and in particular to its pastoral importance as a permanent vocation. THE Scriptures tell us of Saint Stephen and his fellow deacons who ministered to the Church at Jerusalem. They served as co-workers of the bishop and his body of priests. Today, likewise, the deacons of the Church have a special role to fulfill. They assist the bishop, first of all, as ministers of the word. They proclaim the Gospel at the liturgy and may be assigned to preach the homily. THEY preside over community prayer and minister at the rite of baptism. They assist at marriages and pronounce God's blessing over the newly wedded couple. To the dying they provide spiritual nourishment in administering holy communion. They lead in the rites of Christian burial. ❖ ❖ ❖ ❖ ❖ ❖ ❖ ❖ ❖ ❖ ❖ ❖ ❖ ❖ ❖

SANCTIFIED for his ministry by the laying on of hands, the deacon is bound very closely to the altar. It is there that he prepares the ❖ ❖ gifts to be offered in the eucharist. From the altar he gives to Christ's people the holy ❖ ❖ ❖ bread and cup of blessing. ❖ ❖ ❖ ❖ ❖ ❖ ❖ ❖ ❖ ❖ ❖ ❖

THE PASTOR depends upon deacons ❖ ❖ ❖ ❖ to carry out many services of Christian ❖ charity. The deacon is called to various ❖ ❖ administrative duties in his parish, where he serves the needs of all in humility. ❖ ❖ ❖ ❖ Whether married or single, he devotes himself generously to the Church which has called ❖ ❖ him to a life of pastoral concern. ❖ ❖ ❖ ❖ ❖ ❖ ❖

The Sacrament of HOLY ORDERS

celebrated in our Family:

DIACONATE

DEACON

Name _____

ORDINATION

Date _____

Ordaining Bishop _____

Church _____

City _____ State _____

KEEP·WATCH +

over the whole flock
the Holy Spirit has
given you. Shepherd
the church of God. +

ACTS 20:28

TRULY, THE ENTIRE PEOPLE OF GOD are a priestly community. Through ❖ ❖ ❖ baptismal water and sacred chrism they ❖ are sacramentally one with Christ the Priest. Together with him they offer eucharist. But the Lord also chooses some of his disciples to serve publicly as spiritual leaders of the congregation. The special consecration into the priestly community bestows a threefold ❖ blessing of the Spirit. ❖ ❖ ❖ ❖ ❖ ❖ ❖ ❖ ❖ ❖ ❖ ❖ ❖ ❖ ❖

THE priest, as co-worker of his bishop, is a teacher. He is called to preach the Gospel, to share with all peoples the word of ❖ ❖ God he has received with joy. His life, then, is devoted to meditating on the divine law so that he might nourish the minds of all believers. His doctrine is the teaching of ❖

Jesus, and this he shares with all who ❖ ❖ ❖
hunger for the bread of the Scriptures. ❖ ❖
AT divine worship the priest presides. ❖ ❖
With living faith and devotion he leads his
people in prayer. He completes the spiritual
sacrifice of the faithful by uniting it to the
heavenly oblation of the Risen Christ. He
summons them to join with him in hallow-
ing the hours of the day with psalms and
spiritual canticles. He forms his people into
a liturgical assembly. ❖ ❖ ❖ ❖ ❖ ❖ ❖ ❖ ❖ ❖ ❖ ❖ ❖
FINALLY, the priest is a shepherd of the
flock. He desires to convert a crowd into a
community, bringing all together as a ❖ ❖ ❖
unified family. He remembers the example
of Christ the Good Shepherd, who came ❖ ❖
not to be served but to serve, to seek out ❖ ❖
those who are lost. ❖ ❖ ❖ ❖ ❖ ❖ ❖ ❖ ❖ ❖ ❖ ❖ ❖

The Sacrament of HOLY ORDERS celebrated in our Family: PRIESTHOOD

A PRIEST FOREVER

Name _____

ORDINATION

Date _____

Ordaining Bishop _____

Church _____

City _____ State _____

FIRST MASS

Date _____

Assistant Priest _____

Preacher _____

Church _____

City _____ State _____

FOR THIS REASON
a man shall leave his
father and mother and
shall be joined to his wife,
AND THE TWO SHALL
BE MADE INTO ONE.

EPHESIANS 5:31

WITH THE ANCIENT PSALMIST we sing of holy parenthood: "Your wife is like a fruitful vine within your house; ❖ ❖ your children are like shoots of the olive tree around your table." ❖ ❖ ❖ ❖ ❖ ❖ ❖ ❖ ❖ ❖ ❖ ❖ ❖ AS sons and daughters grow gradually to maturity, they begin to reflect upon their future. Eventually they choose their states in life. Almost before parents are ready for it, their children are prepared to take the very step they themselves took years before. They are now ready to leave father and mother, to unite with their own spouses, and in ❖ turn to bring forth human life into the world. Their children, too, will one day turn to Mother Church, who through the centuries engenders divine life within all who turn to her as disciples of the Lord. ❖ ❖ ❖ ❖ ❖ ❖ ❖ ❖ ❖ ❖

THERE is a new joy for Christian parents in the wedding of their daughter or son. It is a spiritual marriage in Christ. The grace of the sacrament will accompany the ❖❖❖ young person throughout life. The Lord ❖❖ lays his hands of blessing upon the wedding couple, ennobling their mutual love, ❖❖❖❖ spiritualizing the ministry that shall be theirs as mother and father. Every Christian ❖❖❖❖ vocation is a special charism of the Spirit, calling a disciple of Jesus to become a saint in this world, a member of the household of God.

IN the rite of baptism, one is summoned to the altar of the parish church, there to begin a new life of holiness. And now there is a ❖ return to that altar in a procession of special dedication: a covenant of love shall be ❖❖❖ celebrated by a woman and a man. A new family is about to enter history. ❖❖❖❖❖❖❖

The Sacrament of MARRIAGE celebrated in our Family

Groom _____

Bride _____

Minister _____

Best Man _____

Bridesmaid _____

Date _____ Church _____

City _____ State _____

Groom _____

Bride _____

Minister _____

Best Man _____

Bridesmaid _____

Date _____ Church _____

City _____ State _____

Groom _____

Bride _____

Minister _____

Best Man _____

Bridesmaid _____

Date _____ Church _____

City _____ State _____

Groom _____

Bride _____

Minister _____

Best Man _____

Bridesmaid _____

Date _____ Church _____

City _____ State _____

Groom _____

Bride _____

Minister _____

Best Man _____

Bridesmaid _____

Date _____ Church _____

City _____ State _____

Groom _____

Bride _____

Minister _____

Best Man _____

Bridesmaid _____

Date _____ Church _____

City _____ State _____

Wedding Photographs

Wedding Photographs

71

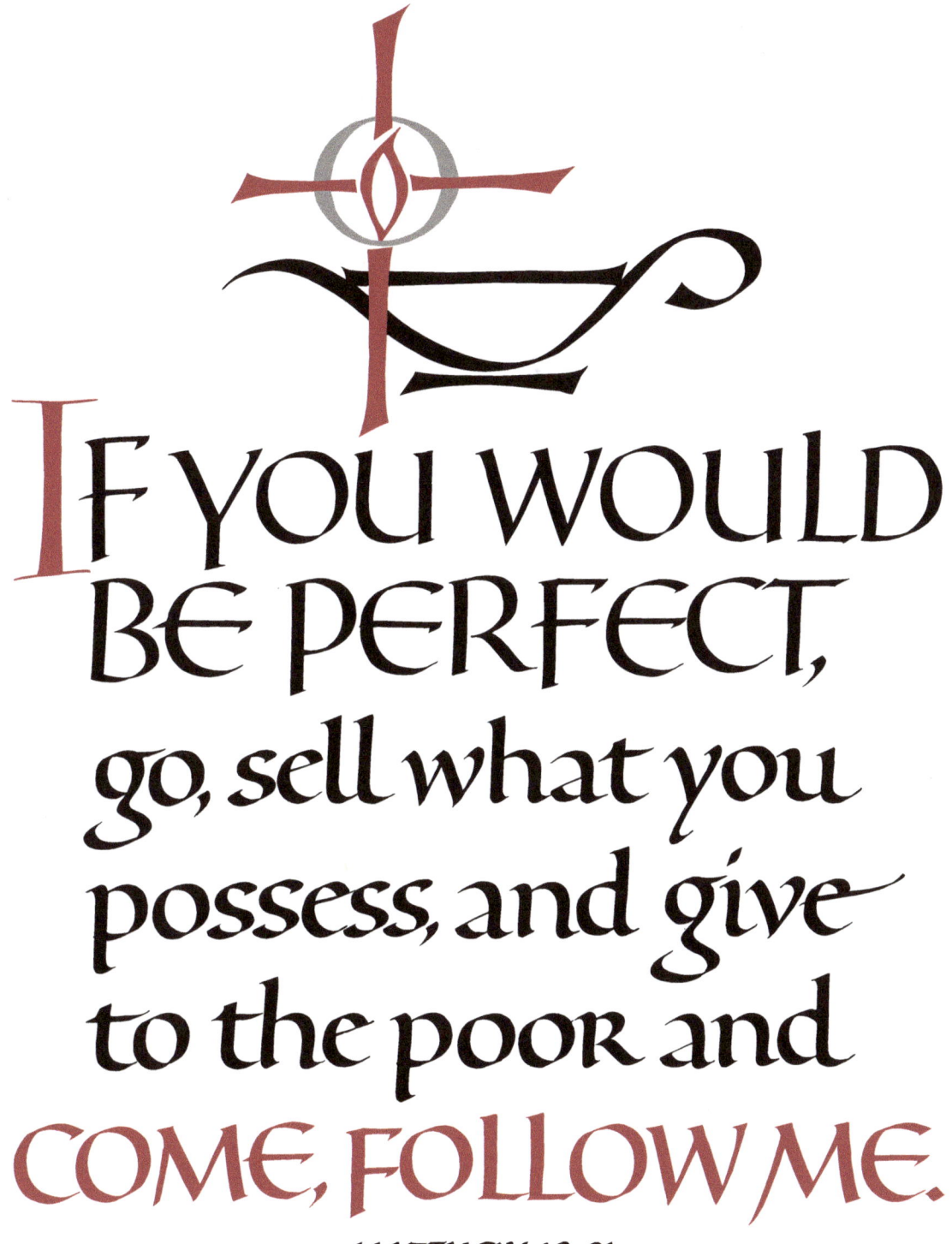

If you would be perfect,

go, sell what you possess, and give to the poor and

COME, FOLLOW ME.

MATTHEW 19:21

IN EVERY AGE OF HUMAN HISTORY, Jesus continues to call his disciples to a life of faith and ministry to others. Each Christian, whether married or single, has answered this vocation in one way or another. Among those who remain in the single state, some have received a special calling to enter spiritual ❖ ❖ communities dedicated, uniquely and single-heartedly, to prayer and specific works of Christian service. ❖ ❖ ❖ ❖ ❖ ❖ ❖ ❖ ❖ ❖ ❖ ❖ ❖ ❖ ❖

THERE are countless different religious ❖ ❖ ❖ orders in the Church, each with its own spirit and its own form of apostolate. Their founders were holy men and women whose lives were absorbed in prayer and zeal for the Gospel. ❖ Some of these orders are more especially ❖ ❖ intended to carry out the Church's ❖ ❖ ❖ ❖ ❖ contemplative vocation. They lead a life of interior recollection and radical withdrawal from secular society. Others combine a daily prayer-life with civic and social works of ❖ ❖ charity, mingling industriously with the ❖ ❖ needs and opportunities of this world's affairs.

THE religious call is a source of joy for parents, and a precious fruit of Christian family life. It gives evidence of Christ's special blessing ❖ ❖ on the family. Those who are so chosen leave their homes and families in order to live in ❖ closer union with Christ and his Church. ❖ ❖ Through their profession of vows they indeed enter another family. ❖ ❖ ❖ ❖ ❖ ❖ ❖ ❖ ❖ ❖ ❖ ❖ ❖

THE religious community, due to its outward ❖ form and inner purposes, is meant to be a sign to the world of spiritual values it is ever in danger of forgetting. Such a community is ❖ ❖ dedicated to witness as a more perfect ❖ ❖ ❖ ❖ ❖ miniature of the Church universal. ❖ ❖ ❖ ❖ ❖ ❖

The Life of Christ's COUNSELS embraced in Religious Life in our Family

Christian Name _____

Name in Religion _____

Entrance into Novitiate _____

First Profession _____

Perpetual Profession _____

Place _____

City _____ State _____

Christian Name _____

Name in Religion _____

Entrance into Novitiate _____

First Profession _____

Perpetual Profession _____

Place _____

City _____ State _____

ALL·THOSE·WHO
BELIEVE·IN·ME,
though they should die,
will come to life. JOHN 11:26

ALL THE CHRISTIAN LITURGIES celebrate the Paschal Mystery of the Risen Lord. But none does it more beautifully than the rite of Christian burial. Already in baptism we were buried with him and rose with him. But in the funeral rites the passing over from death to life reaches its final and glorious phase. PURIFIED in soul and welcomed into the fellowship of the saints in heaven, the Christian pilgrim moves on now from mortality to immortality. In celebrating the solemn rites of burial, the family of God affirms its confidence in eternal life. It looks forward in blessed hope to the Lord's final coming and the bodily resurrection of the dead.

THE bodies of the faithful departed have been temples of the Holy Spirit. We honor them and give them our marks of respect. Though we are saddened by death and ❖ ❖ stunned by its mystery, we look upon the enigma with eyes of faith. To those whose gaze is fixed upon the things of this world only, death is indeed meaningless. But to the Christian family it appears as an ❖ ❖ ❖ entrance into glory and a source of ❖ ❖ ❖ ❖ ❖ profound consolation. ❖ ❖ ❖ ❖ ❖ ❖ ❖ ❖ ❖ ❖ ❖ ❖ ❖

THUS do the sacred rites come to their ❖ close upon earth. Are not all of our ❖ ❖ ❖ sacraments a wondrous sharing in the ❖ life of heaven? John the Apostle declares to us: "We are even now children of God. ❖ What we are next to become is not apparent yet. But we do know that when He appears we are to be like Him. For we shall see ❖ ❖ Him as He is." ❖ ❖ ❖ ❖ ❖ ❖ ❖ ❖ ❖ ❖ ❖ ❖ ❖ ❖ ❖ ❖ ❖

Laid to rest
IN THE PEACE AND LOVE OF CHRIST

Name of Father_____

FELL ASLEEP IN THE LORD AND WAS LAID TO
REST IN THE PEACE AND LOVE OF CHRIST.

Death_____ Burial_____

Cemetery_____

City_____ State_____

Name of Mother_____

FELL ASLEEP IN THE LORD AND WAS LAID TO
REST IN THE PEACE AND LOVE OF CHRIST.

Death_____ Burial_____

Cemetery_____

City_____ State_____

Name_____
FELL ASLEEP IN THE LORD AND WAS LAID TO
REST IN THE PEACE AND LOVE OF CHRIST.

Death_____ Burial_____

Cemetery_____

City_____ State_____

Name_____
FELL ASLEEP IN THE LORD AND WAS LAID TO
REST IN THE PEACE AND LOVE OF CHRIST.

Death_____ Burial_____

Cemetery_____

City_____ State_____

Name_____
FELL ASLEEP IN THE LORD AND WAS LAID TO
REST IN THE PEACE AND LOVE OF CHRIST.

Death_____ Burial_____

Cemetery_____

City_____ State_____

Name_____
FELL ASLEEP IN THE LORD AND WAS LAID TO
REST IN THE PEACE AND LOVE OF CHRIST.

Death_____ Burial_____

Cemetery_____

City_____ State_____

Name_____
FELL ASLEEP IN THE LORD AND WAS LAID TO
REST IN THE PEACE AND LOVE OF CHRIST.

Death_____ Burial_____

Cemetery_____

City_____ State_____

Name_____
FELL ASLEEP IN THE LORD AND WAS LAID TO
REST IN THE PEACE AND LOVE OF CHRIST.

Death_____ Burial_____

Cemetery_____

City_____ State_____

May our Lord Jesus Christ who loved us
and through grace gave us eternal comfort
and good hope, comfort your hearts.

2 THESSALONIANS 2:16-17

PARENTS MAY OCCASIONALLY EXPERIENCE
the loss of their infant without the opportunity
of its being reborn in baptism. Divine providence
alone is fully able to understand this mystery.
But Christian families find consolation and ❖
encouragement in their faith. At such a ❖❖❖
difficult hour father and mother turn to God
in confident hope and trust. God's wisdom, ❖
the Scriptures declare, is greater than ours, and ❖❖
Gods love is mightier than death. We place our
hope in Christ the Living One, who died for us all.

ONE of the principal purposes of baptism is to give entrance to membership in the Church; it is a rite of initiation. But to those unbaptized infants whom God has lovingly called to himself beyond this earthly life there is offered a higher and more final initiation: entrance into the eternal joys of the Lord. Although God ordinarily has bound our salvation to the sacrament of baptism, God is not limited by the sacraments he has given us.

IN his powerful resurrection Christ leads his church beyond sacraments, beyond liturgical rites, beyond faith itself. The sights of this present world are left behind, and the vision of God appears.

Name_____

Date of Birth_____

Date of Death_____

Place of Burial_____

City_____State_____

OUR FAMILY

OUR HUMAN ANCESTRY IS A pervasive dimension of who we are as persons. Our human roots have helped to shape, guide, and influence our growth to maturity in a particular human family. They are important in making us the special kind of persons we are.

AND it is the special kind of persons that we are that our loving God calls and makes members of God's own family. After we are born into a human family we are reborn through baptism into the family of God. God writes our names in the Book of Life. For this reason a genealogical section is included in this Family Book of Life to allow you to record your human family, the family that God incorporates into the heavenly Book of Life.

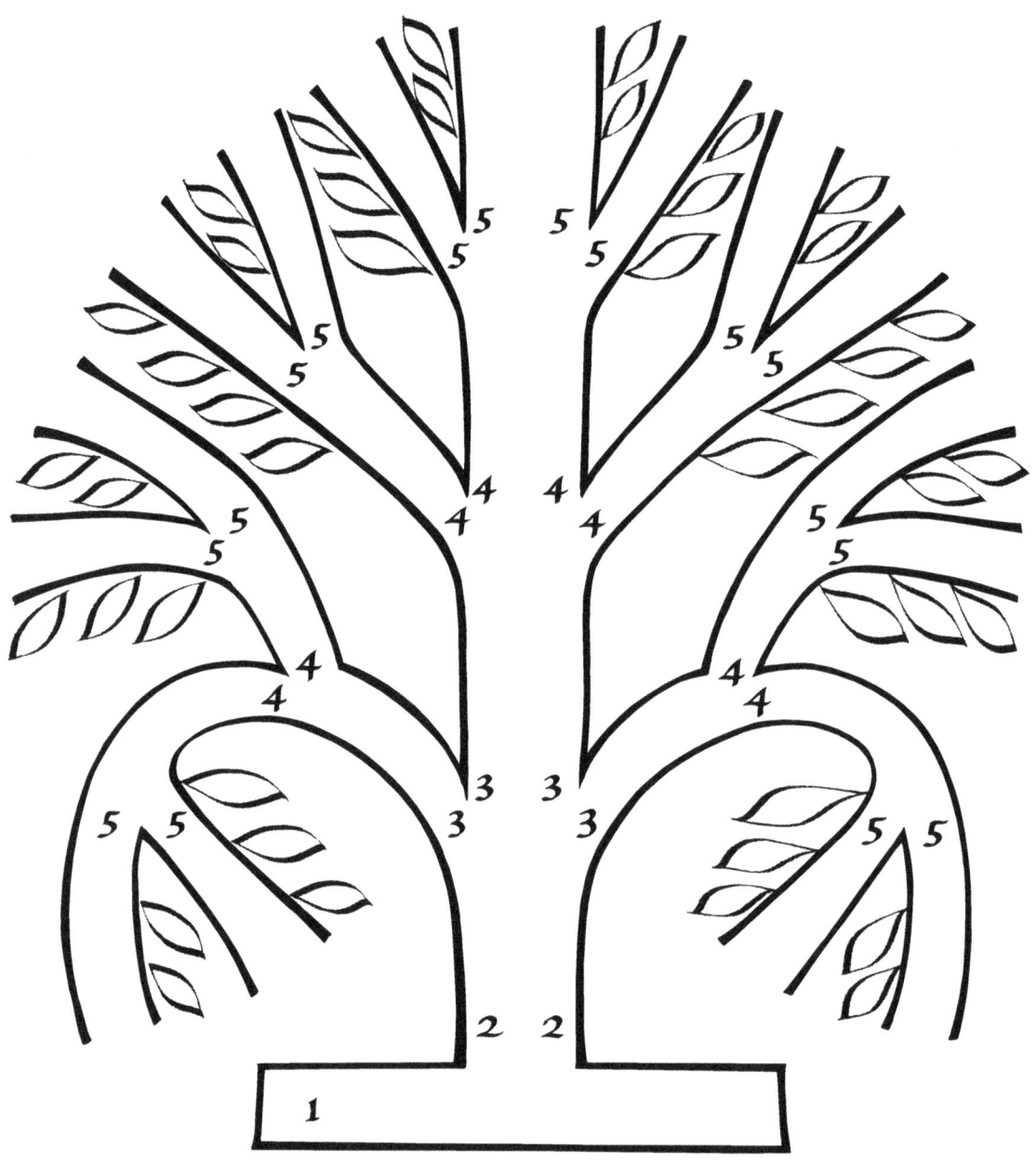

DIRECTIONS FOR FAMILY TREE
Write the name of the oldest child or your name at number 1 at the base of the tree. At the spaces marked 2 write the names of parents; 3, names of grandparents, and so on.

Our Family

	WIFE		HUSBAND
		NAME	
		BORN	
		MARRIED	
		DIED	
		BURIAL	
		FATHER	
		MOTHER	

NOTES

	Sex	Children in order of birth	BORN day month year	Place of birth	DIED day month year
1					
DATE MARRIED		SPOUSE			
2					
DATE MARRIED		SPOUSE			
3					
DATE MARRIED		SPOUSE			
4					
DATE MARRIED		SPOUSE			
5					
DATE MARRIED		SPOUSE			
6					
DATE MARRIED		SPOUSE			
7					
DATE MARRIED		SPOUSE			
8					
DATE MARRIED		SPOUSE			

Children / Grandchildren

WIFE			HUSBAND	
		NAME		
		BORN		
		MARRIED		
		DIED		
		BURIAL		

	Sex	Children in order of birth	BORN day month year	Place of birth	DIED day month year
1					
DATE MARRIED		SPOUSE			
2					
DATE MARRIED		SPOUSE			
3					
DATE MARRIED		SPOUSE			
4					
DATE MARRIED		SPOUSE			

WIFE			HUSBAND	
		NAME		
		BORN		
		MARRIED		
		DIED		
		BURIAL		

	Sex	Children in order of birth	BORN day month year	Place of birth	DIED day month year
1					
DATE MARRIED		SPOUSE			
2					
DATE MARRIED		SPOUSE			
3					
DATE MARRIED		SPOUSE			
4					
DATE MARRIED		SPOUSE			

Children / Grandchildren

WIFE			HUSBAND	

	NAME			
	BORN			
	MARRIED			
	DIED			
	BURIAL			

	Sex	Children in order of birth	BORN day month year	Place of birth	DIED day month year
1					
DATE MARRIED		SPOUSE			
2					
DATE MARRIED		SPOUSE			
3					
DATE MARRIED		SPOUSE			
4					
DATE MARRIED		SPOUSE			

WIFE			HUSBAND	

	NAME			
	BORN			
	MARRIED			
	DIED			
	BURIAL			

	Sex	Children in order of birth	BORN day month year	Place of birth	DIED day month year
1					
DATE MARRIED		SPOUSE			
2					
DATE MARRIED		SPOUSE			
3					
DATE MARRIED		SPOUSE			
4					
DATE MARRIED		SPOUSE			

Children / Grandchildren

WIFE			HUSBAND	

	NAME	
	BORN	
	MARRIED	
	DIED	
	BURIAL	

	Sex	Children in order of birth	BORN day month year	Place of birth	DIED day month year
1					
DATE MARRIED	SPOUSE				
2					
DATE MARRIED	SPOUSE				
3					
DATE MARRIED	SPOUSE				
4					
DATE MARRIED	SPOUSE				

WIFE			HUSBAND	

	NAME	
	BORN	
	MARRIED	
	DIED	
	BURIAL	

	Sex	Children in order of birth	BORN day month year	Place of birth	DIED day month year
1					
DATE MARRIED	SPOUSE				
2					
DATE MARRIED	SPOUSE				
3					
DATE MARRIED	SPOUSE				
4					
DATE MARRIED	SPOUSE				

Family Photograph

The Children's Grandparents PATERNAL

	WIFE	HUSBAND
NAME		
BORN		
MARRIED		
DIED		
BURIAL		
FATHER		
MOTHER		

NOTES

	Sex	Children in order of birth	BORN day month year	Place of birth	DIED day month year
1					
DATE MARRIED	SPOUSE				
2					
DATE MARRIED	SPOUSE				
3					
DATE MARRIED	SPOUSE				
4					
DATE MARRIED	SPOUSE				
5					
DATE MARRIED	SPOUSE				
6					
DATE MARRIED	SPOUSE				
7					
DATE MARRIED	SPOUSE				
8					
DATE MARRIED	SPOUSE				

The Children's Grandparents MATERNAL

WIFE	HUSBAND
	NAME
	BORN
	MARRIED
	DIED
	BURIAL
	FATHER
	MOTHER

NOTES

	Sex	Children in order of birth	BORN day month year	Place of birth	DIED day month year
1					
DATE MARRIED		SPOUSE			
2					
DATE MARRIED		SPOUSE			
3					
DATE MARRIED		SPOUSE			
4					
DATE MARRIED		SPOUSE			
5					
DATE MARRIED		SPOUSE			
6					
DATE MARRIED		SPOUSE			
7					
DATE MARRIED		SPOUSE			
8					
DATE MARRIED		SPOUSE			

The Children's Great Grandparents PATERNAL

	WIFE	HUSBAND
NAME		
BORN		
MARRIED		
DIED		
BURIAL		
FATHER		
MOTHER		

NOTES

	Sex	Children in order of birth	BORN day month year	Place of birth	DIED day month year
1					
DATE MARRIED	SPOUSE				
2					
DATE MARRIED	SPOUSE				
3					
DATE MARRIED	SPOUSE				
4					
DATE MARRIED	SPOUSE				
5					
DATE MARRIED	SPOUSE				
6					
DATE MARRIED	SPOUSE				
7					
DATE MARRIED	SPOUSE				
8					
DATE MARRIED	SPOUSE				

The Children's Great Grandparents PATERNAL

	WIFE		HUSBAND
		NAME	
		BORN	
		MARRIED	
		DIED	
		BURIAL	
		FATHER	
		MOTHER	

NOTES

	Sex	Children in order of birth	BORN day month year	Place of birth	DIED day month year
1					
DATE MARRIED	SPOUSE				
2					
DATE MARRIED	SPOUSE				
3					
DATE MARRIED	SPOUSE				
4					
DATE MARRIED	SPOUSE				
5					
DATE MARRIED	SPOUSE				
6					
DATE MARRIED	SPOUSE				
7					
DATE MARRIED	SPOUSE				
8					
DATE MARRIED	SPOUSE				

The Children's Great Grandparents MATERNAL

	WIFE	HUSBAND
NAME		
BORN		
MARRIED		
DIED		
BURIAL		
FATHER		
MOTHER		

NOTES

	Sex	Children in order of birth	BORN day month year	Place of birth	DIED day month year
1					
	DATE MARRIED	SPOUSE			
2					
	DATE MARRIED	SPOUSE			
3					
	DATE MARRIED	SPOUSE			
4					
	DATE MARRIED	SPOUSE			
5					
	DATE MARRIED	SPOUSE			
6					
	DATE MARRIED	SPOUSE			
7					
	DATE MARRIED	SPOUSE			
8					
	DATE MARRIED	SPOUSE			

The Children's Great Grandparents MATERNAL

	WIFE	HUSBAND
NAME		
BORN		
MARRIED		
DIED		
BURIAL		
FATHER		
MOTHER		

NOTES

	Sex	Children in order of birth	BORN day month year	Place of birth	DIED day month year
1					
DATE MARRIED	SPOUSE				
2					
DATE MARRIED	SPOUSE				
3					
DATE MARRIED	SPOUSE				
4					
DATE MARRIED	SPOUSE				
5					
DATE MARRIED	SPOUSE				
6					
DATE MARRIED	SPOUSE				
7					
DATE MARRIED	SPOUSE				
8					
DATE MARRIED	SPOUSE				

Ancestral Chart of Father

1 _____
   FATHER

Place the full name
of father on line 1.
Lines 2 and 3 are
father and mother
of line 1, etc. Use
full maiden name
for all women.

2 _____
BORN _____
WHERE _____
DATE OF MARRIAGE _____
DIED _____
WHERE _____

3 _____
BORN _____
WHERE _____
DIED _____
WHERE _____

4 _____
BORN _____
WHERE _____
DATE OF MARRIAGE _____
DIED _____
WHERE _____

5 _____
BORN _____
WHERE _____
DIED _____
WHERE _____

6 _____
BORN _____
WHERE _____
DATE OF MARRIAGE _____
DIED _____
WHERE _____

7 _____
BORN _____
WHERE _____
DIED _____
WHERE _____

8 _____
BORN _____ WHERE _____
DATE OF MARRIAGE _____
DIED _____ WHERE _____

9 _____
BORN _____ WHERE _____
DIED _____ WHERE _____

10 _____
BORN _____ WHERE _____
DATE OF MARRIAGE _____
DIED _____ WHERE _____

11 _____
BORN _____ WHERE _____
DIED _____ WHERE _____

12 _____
BORN _____ WHERE _____
DATE OF MARRIAGE _____
DIED _____ WHERE _____

13 _____
BORN _____ WHERE _____
DIED _____ WHERE _____

14 _____
BORN _____ WHERE _____
DATE OF MARRIAGE _____
DIED _____ WHERE _____

15 _____
BORN _____ WHERE _____
DIED _____ WHERE _____

Ancestral Chart of Mother

1 MOTHER

Place the full name of mother on line 1. Lines 2 and 3 are father and mother of line 1, etc. Use full maiden name for all women.

2
BORN
WHERE
DATE OF MARRIAGE
DIED
WHERE

3
BORN
WHERE
DIED
WHERE

4
BORN
WHERE
DATE OF MARRIAGE
DIED
WHERE

5
BORN
WHERE
DIED
WHERE

6
BORN
WHERE
DATE OF MARRIAGE
DIED
WHERE

7
BORN
WHERE
DIED
WHERE

8
BORN
DATE OF MARRIAGE
DIED
WHERE
WHERE

9
BORN
DIED
WHERE
WHERE

10
BORN
DATE OF MARRIAGE
DIED
WHERE
WHERE

11
BORN
DIED
WHERE
WHERE

12
BORN
DATE OF MARRIAGE
DIED
WHERE
WHERE

13
BORN
DIED
WHERE
WHERE

14
BORN
DATE OF MARRIAGE
DIED
WHERE
WHERE

15
BORN
DIED
WHERE
WHERE

NOTHING profane shall enter the heavenly Jerusalem. Only those shall enter whose names are inscribed in THE BOOK OF LIFE kept by the Lamb.

REVELATION 21:27

CPSIA information can be obtained
at www.ICGtesting.com
Printed in the USA
BVHW020514120422
633857BV00002B/16